Congregation for the Doctrine of the Faith

The Dignity of a Person

Dignitas Personae

WITH ADDITIONAL RESOURCES

United States Conference of Catholic Bishops
Washington, D.C.

Publication No. 7-069
United States Conference of Catholic Bishops
Washington, D.C.
ISBN 978-1-60137-069-3
Published in the United States, February 2009

Contents

Part I

THE DIGNITY
OF A PERSON

DIGNITAS PERSONAE

Instruction *Dignitas Personae* on Certain Bioethical Questions

Congregation for the Doctrine of the Faith

Introduction

1. The dignity of a person must be recognized in every human being from conception to natural death. This fundamental principle expresses *a great "yes" to human life* and must be at the center of ethical reflection on biomedical research, which has an ever greater importance in today's world. The Church's Magisterium has frequently intervened to clarify and resolve moral questions in this area. The Instruction *Donum Vitae* was particularly significant.[1] And now, twenty years after its publication, it is appropriate to bring it up to date.

The teaching of *Donum Vitae* remains completely valid, both with regard to the principles on which it is based and the moral evaluations which it expresses. However, new biomedical technologies which have been introduced in the critical area of human life and the family have given rise to further questions, in particular in the field of research on human embryos, the use of stem cells for therapeutic purposes, as well as in other areas of experimental medicine.

---

1   CONGREGATION FOR THE DOCTRINE OF THE FAITH, Instruction *Donum Vitae* on respect for human life at its origins and for the dignity of procreation (22 February 1987): AAS 80 (1988), 70-102.

These new questions require answers. The pace of scientific developments in this area and the publicity they have received have raised expectations and concerns in large sectors of public opinion. Legislative assemblies have been asked to make decisions on these questions in order to regulate them by law; at times, wider popular consultation has also taken place.

These developments have led the Congregation for the Doctrine of the Faith to prepare *a new doctrinal Instruction* which addresses some recent questions in the light of the criteria expressed in the Instruction *Donum Vitae* and which also examines some issues that were treated earlier, but are in need of additional clarification.

2. In undertaking this study, the Congregation for the Doctrine of the Faith has benefited from the analysis of the Pontifical Academy for Life and has consulted numerous experts with regard to the scientific aspects of these questions, in order to address them with the principles of Christian anthropology. The Encyclicals *Veritatis Splendor*[2] and *Evangelium Vitae*[3] of John Paul II, as well as other interventions of the Magisterium, offer clear indications with regard to both the method and the content of the examination of the problems under consideration.

---

2   JOHN PAUL II, Encyclical Letter *Veritatis Splendor* regarding certain fundamental questions of the Church's moral teaching (6 August 1993): AAS 85 (1993), 1133-1228.

3   JOHN PAUL II, Encyclical Letter *Evangelium Vitae* on the value and inviolability of human life (25 March 1995): AAS 87 (1995), 401-522.

In the current multifaceted philosophical and scientific context, a considerable number of scientists and philosophers, in the spirit of the *Hippocratic Oath*, see in medical science a service to human fragility aimed at the cure of disease, the relief of suffering and the equitable extension of necessary care to all people. At the same time, however, there are also persons in the world of philosophy and science who view advances in biomedical technology from an essentially eugenic perspective.

3. In presenting principles and moral evaluations regarding biomedical research on human life, the Catholic Church draws upon *the light both of reason and of faith* and seeks to set forth an integral vision of man and his vocation, capable of incorporating everything that is good in human activity, as well as in various cultural and religious traditions which not infrequently demonstrate a great reverence for life.

The Magisterium also seeks to offer a word of support and encouragement for the perspective on culture which considers *science an invaluable service to the integral good of the life and dignity of every human being.* The Church therefore views scientific research with hope and desires that many Christians will dedicate themselves to the progress of biomedicine and will bear witness to their faith in this field. She hopes moreover that the results of such research may also be made available in areas of the world that are poor and afflicted by disease, so that those who are most in need will receive humanitarian assistance. Finally, the Church seeks to draw near to every human being who is suffering, whether in body or in spirit, in order to bring not only comfort, but also light and hope. These give meaning to moments of sickness and to the experience of death, which indeed are part of human life and are present in the story of every person, opening that story to the mystery of the Resurrection. Truly, the gaze of the Church is full of trust because "life will triumph: this is a sure hope for us. Yes, life will triumph because truth, goodness, joy and true progress are on the side of life. God, who loves life and gives it generously, is on the side of life."[4]

The present Instruction is addressed to the Catholic faithful and to all who seek the truth.[5] It has three parts: the first recalls some anthropological, theological and ethical elements of fundamental importance; the second addresses new problems regarding procreation; the third examines new procedures involving the manipulation of embryos and the human genetic patrimony.

---

4   JOHN PAUL II, Address to the participants in the Seventh Assembly of the Pontifical Academy of Life (3 March 2001), 3: AAS 93 (2001), 446.

5   Cf. JOHN PAUL II, Encyclical Letter *Fides et Ratio* on the relationship between faith and reason (14 September 1998), 1: AAS 91 (1999), 5.

First Part:
Anthropological, Theological and Ethical Aspects of Human Life and Procreation

4. In recent decades, medical science has made significant strides in understanding human life in its initial stages. Human biological structures and the process of human generation are better known. These developments are certainly positive and worthy of support when they serve to overcome or correct pathologies and succeed in re-establishing the normal functioning of human procreation. On the other hand, they are negative and cannot be utilized when they involve the destruction of human beings or when they employ means which contradict the dignity of the person or when they are used for purposes contrary to the integral good of man.

The body of a human being, from the very first stages of its existence, can never be reduced merely to a group of cells. The embryonic human body develops progressively according to a well-defined program with its proper finality, as is apparent in the birth of every baby.

It is appropriate to recall the *fundamental ethical criterion* expressed in the Instruction *Donum Vitae* in order to evaluate all moral questions which relate to procedures involving the human embryo: "Thus the fruit of human generation, from the first moment of its existence, that is to say, from the moment the zygote has formed, demands the unconditional respect that is morally due to the human being in his bodily and spiritual totality. The human being is to be respected and treated as a person from the moment of conception; and therefore from that same moment his rights as a person must be recognized, among which in the first place is the inviolable right of every innocent human being to life."[6]

5. This ethical principle, which reason is capable of recognizing as true and in conformity with the natural moral law, should be the basis for all legislation in this area.[7] In fact, it presupposes a *truth of an ontological character*, as *Donum Vitae* demonstrated from solid scientific evidence, regarding the continuity in development of a human being.

If *Donum Vitae*, in order to avoid a statement of an explicitly philosophical nature, did not define the embryo as a person, it nonetheless did indicate that there is an intrinsic connection between the ontological dimension and the specific value of every human life. Although the presence of the spiritual soul cannot be observed experimentally, the conclusions of science regarding the human embryo give "a valuable indication for discerning by the use of reason a personal presence at the moment of the first appearance of a human life: how could a human individual not be a

---

6 Congregation for the Doctrine of the Faith, Instruction *Donum Vitae*, I, 1: *AAS* 80 (1988), 79.

7 Human rights, as Pope Benedict XVI has recalled, and in particular the right to life of every human being "are based on the natural law inscribed on human hearts and present in different cultures and civilizations. Removing human rights from this context would mean restricting their range and yielding to a relativistic conception, according to which the meaning and interpretation of rights could vary and their universality would be denied in the name of different cultural, political, social and even religious outlooks. This great variety of viewpoints must not be allowed to obscure the fact that not only rights are universal, but so too is the human person, the subject of those rights" (Address to the General Assembly of the United Nations [18 April 2008]: *AAS* 100 [2008], 334).

human person?"[8] Indeed, the reality of the human being for the entire span of life, both before and after birth, does not allow us to posit either a change in nature or a gradation in moral value, since it possesses *full anthropological and ethical status*. The human embryo has, therefore, from the very beginning, the dignity proper to a person.

6. Respect for that dignity is owed to every human being because each one carries in an indelible way his own dignity and value. *The origin of human life has its authentic context in marriage and in the family*, where it is generated through an act which expresses the reciprocal love between a man and a woman. Procreation which is truly responsible vis-à-vis the child to be born "must be the fruit of marriage."[9]

Marriage, present in all times and in all cultures, "is in reality something wisely and providently instituted by God the Creator with a view to carrying out his loving plan in human beings. Thus, husband and wife, through the reciprocal gift of themselves to the other—something which is proper and exclusive to them—bring about that communion of persons by which they perfect each other, so as to cooperate with God in the procreation and raising of new lives."[10] In the fruitfulness of married love, man and woman "make it clear that at the origin of their spousal life there is a genuine 'yes,' which is pronounced and truly lived in reciprocity, remaining ever open to life. . . . Natural law, which is at

---

8   Congregation for the Doctrine of the Faith, Instruction *Donum Vitae*, I, 1: AAS 80 (1988), 78-79.

9   Congregation for the Doctrine of the Faith, Instruction *Donum Vitae*, II, A, 1: AAS 80 (1988), 87.

10 Paul VI, Encyclical Letter *Humanae Vitae* (25 July 1968), n. 8: AAS 60 (1968), 485-486.

the root of the recognition of true equality between persons and peoples, deserves to be recognized as the source that inspires the relationship between the spouses in their responsibility for begetting new children. The transmission of life is inscribed in nature and its laws stand as an unwritten norm to which all must refer."[11]

7. It is the Church's conviction that what is human is not only received and respected by *faith*, but is also purified, elevated and perfected. God, after having created man in his image and likeness (cf. Gn 1:26), described his creature as "very good" (Gn 1:31), so as to be assumed later in the Son (cf. Jn 1:14). In the mystery of the Incarnation, the Son of God confirmed the dignity of the body and soul which constitute the human being. Christ did not disdain human bodiliness, but instead fully disclosed its meaning and value: "In reality, it is only in the mystery of the incarnate Word that the mystery of man truly becomes clear."[12]

By becoming one of us, the Son makes it possible for us to become "sons of God" (Jn 1:12), "sharers in the divine nature" (2 Pt 1:4). This new dimension does not conflict with the dignity of the creature which everyone can recognize by the use of reason, but elevates it into a wider horizon of life which is proper to God, giving us the ability to reflect

---

11 BENEDICT XVI, Address to the Participants in the International Congress organized by the Pontifical Lateran University on the Fortieth Anniversary of the Encyclical *Humanae Vitae*, 10 May 2008: *L'Osservatore Romano*, 11 May 2008, 1; cf. John XXIII, Encyclical Letter *Mater et Magistra* (15 May 1961), III: AAS 53 (1961), 447.

12 SECOND VATICAN COUNCIL, Pastoral Constitution *Gaudium et Spes*, n. 22.

more profoundly on human life and on the acts by which it is brought into existence.[13]

The respect for the individual human being, which reason requires, is further enhanced and strengthened in the light of these truths of faith: thus, we see that there is no contradiction between the affirmation of the dignity and the affirmation of the sacredness of human life. "The different ways in which God, acting in history, cares for the world and for mankind are not mutually exclusive; on the contrary, they support each other and intersect. They have their origin and goal in the eternal, wise and loving counsel whereby God predestines men and women 'to be conformed to the image of his Son' (Rom 8:29)."[14]

8. By taking the interrelationship of these two dimensions, *the human and the divine*, as the starting point, one understands better why it is that man has unassailable value: *he possesses an eternal vocation* and *is called to share in the trinitarian love of the living God.*

This value belongs to all without distinction. By virtue of the simple fact of existing, every human being must be fully respected. The introduction of discrimination with regard to human dignity based on biological, psychological, or educational development, or based on health-related criteria, must be excluded. At every stage of his existence, man, created in the image and likeness of God, reflects "the face of his Only-begotten Son. . . . This boundless and almost incomprehensible love of God for the human being reveals

---

13   Cf. JOHN PAUL II, Encyclical Letter *Evangelium Vitae*, nn. 37-38: AAS 87 (1995), 442-444.

14   JOHN PAUL II, Encyclical Letter *Veritatis Splendor*, n. 45: AAS 85 (1993), 1169.

the degree to which the human person deserves to be loved in himself, independently of any other consideration—intelligence, beauty, health, youth, integrity, and so forth. In short, human life is always a good, for it 'is a manifestation of God in the world, a sign of his presence, a trace of his glory' (*Evangelium Vitae*, n. 34)."[15]

9. These two dimensions of life, the natural and the supernatural, allow us to understand better the sense in which *the acts that permit a new human being to come into existence*, in which a man and a woman give themselves to each other, *are a reflection of trinitarian love*. "God, who is love and life, has inscribed in man and woman the vocation to share in a special way in his mystery of personal communion and in his work as Creator and Father."[16]

Christian marriage is rooted "in the natural complementarity that exists between man and woman, and is nurtured through the personal willingness of the spouses to share their entire life-project, what they have and what they are: for this reason such communion is the fruit and the sign of a profoundly human need. But in Christ the Lord, God takes up this human need, confirms it, purifies it and elevates it, leading it to perfection through the sacrament of matrimony: the Holy Spirit who is poured out in the sacramental celebration offers Christian couples the gift of a new communion of love that is the living and real image of

---

15 BENEDICT XVI, Address to the General Assembly of the Pontifical Academy for Life and International Congress on "The Human Embryo in the Preimplantation Phase" (27 February 2006): AAS 98 (2006), 264.

16 CONGREGATION FOR THE DOCTRINE OF THE FAITH, Instruction *Donum Vitae*, Introduction, n. 3: AAS 80 (1988), 75.

that unique unity which makes of the Church the indivisible Mystical Body of the Lord Jesus."[17]

10. The Church, by expressing an ethical judgment on some developments of recent medical research concerning man and his beginnings, does not intervene in the area proper to medical science itself, but rather calls everyone to ethical and social responsibility for their actions. She reminds them that the ethical value of biomedical science is gauged in reference to both the *unconditional respect owed to every human being* at every moment of his or her existence, and the *defense of the specific character of the personal act which transmits life.* The intervention of the Magisterium falls within its mission of *contributing to the formation of conscience,* by authentically teaching the truth which is Christ and at the same time by declaring and confirming authoritatively the principles of the moral order which spring from human nature itself.[18]

---

17 JOHN PAUL II, Apostolic Exhortation *Familiaris Consortio* on the role of the Christian family in the modern world (22 September 1981), n. 19: *AAS* 74 (1982), 101-102.

18 Cf. SECOND VATICAN COUNCIL, Declaration *Dignitatis Humanae,* n. 14.

Second Part:
New Problems
Concerning Procreation

11. In light of the principles recalled above, certain questions regarding procreation which have emerged and have become more clear in the years since the publication of *Donum Vitae* can now be examined.

Techniques for Assisting Fertility

12. With regard to the *treatment of infertility*, new medical techniques must respect three fundamental goods: (a) the right to life and to physical integrity of every human being from conception to natural death; (b) the unity of marriage, which means reciprocal respect for the right within marriage to become a father or mother only together with the other spouse;[19] (c) the specifically human values of sexuality which require "that the procreation of a human person be brought about as the fruit of the conjugal act specific to the love between spouses."[20] Techniques which assist procreation "are not to be rejected on the grounds that they are artificial. As such, they bear witness to the possibilities of the art of medicine. But they must be given a moral evaluation in reference to the dignity of the human person, who

---

19 Cf. Congregation for the Doctrine of the Faith, Instruction *Donum Vitae*, II, A, 1: AAS 80 (1988), 87.

20 Congregation for the Doctrine of the Faith, Instruction *Donum Vitae*, II, B, 4: AAS 80 (1988), 92.

is called to realize his vocation from God to the gift of love and the gift of life."[21]

In light of this principle, all techniques of heterologous artificial fertilization,[22] as well as those techniques of homologous artificial fertilization[23] which substitute for the conjugal act, are to be excluded. On the other hand, techniques which act *as an aid to the conjugal act and its fertility* are permitted. The Instruction *Donum Vitae* states: "The doctor is at the service of persons and of human procreation. He does not have the authority to dispose of them or to decide their fate. A medical intervention respects the dignity of persons when it seeks to assist the conjugal act either in order to facilitate its performance or in order to enable it to achieve its objective once it has been normally performed."[24] And, with regard to homologous artificial insemination, it states: "Homologous artificial insemination within marriage cannot be admitted except for those cases in which the technical means is not a substitute for the conjugal act, but

---

21 CONGREGATION FOR THE DOCTRINE OF THE FAITH, Instruction *Donum Vitae*, Introduction, 3: AAS 80 (1988), 75.

22 The term *heterologous artificial fertilization or procreation* refers to "techniques used to obtain a human conception artificially by the use of gametes coming from at least one donor other than the spouses who are joined in marriage" (Instruction *Donum Vitae*, II: AAS 80 [1988], 86).

23 The term *homologous artificial fertilization or procreation* refers to "the technique used to obtain a human conception using the gametes of the two spouses joined in marriage" (Instruction *Donum Vitae*, II: AAS 80 [1988], 86).

24 CONGREGATION FOR THE DOCTRINE OF THE FAITH, Instruction *Donum Vitae*, II, B, 7: AAS 80 (1988), 96; cf. PIUS XII, Address to those taking part in the Fourth International Congress of Catholic Doctors (29 September 1949): AAS 41 (1949), 560.

serves to facilitate and to help so that the act attains its natural purpose."[25]

13. Certainly, techniques aimed at removing obstacles to natural fertilization, as for example, hormonal treatments for infertility, surgery for endometriosis, unblocking of fallopian tubes or their surgical repair, are licit. All these techniques may be considered *authentic treatments* because, once the problem causing the infertility has been resolved, the married couple is able to engage in conjugal acts resulting in procreation, without the physician's action directly interfering in that act itself. None of these treatments replaces the conjugal act, which alone is worthy of truly responsible procreation.

In order to come to the aid of the many infertile couples who want to have children, *adoption* should be encouraged, promoted and facilitated by appropriate legislation so that the many children who lack parents may receive a home that will contribute to their human development. In addition, research and investment directed at the *prevention of sterility* deserve encouragement.

In Vitro Fertilization and the Deliberate Destruction of Embryos

14. The fact that the process of *in vitro* fertilization very frequently involves the deliberate destruction of embryos was already noted in the Instruction *Donum Vitae*.[26] There were

---

25 CONGREGATION FOR THE DOCTRINE OF THE FAITH, Instruction *Donum Vitae*, II, B, 6: AAS 80 (1988), 94.

26 Cf. CONGREGATION FOR THE DOCTRINE OF THE FAITH, Instruction *Donum Vitae*, II: AAS 80 (1988), 86.

some who maintained that this was due to techniques which were still somewhat imperfect. Subsequent experience has shown, however, that all techniques of *in vitro* fertilization proceed as if the human embryo were simply a mass of cells to be used, selected and discarded.

It is true that approximately a third of women who have recourse to artificial procreation succeed in having a baby. It should be recognized, however, that given the proportion between the total number of embryos produced and those eventually born, *the number of embryos sacrificed is extremely high*.[27] These losses are accepted by the practitioners of *in vitro* fertilization as the price to be paid for positive results. In reality, it is deeply disturbing that research in this area aims principally at obtaining better results in terms of the percentage of babies born to women who begin the process, but does not manifest a concrete interest in the right to life of each individual embryo.

15. It is often objected that the loss of embryos is, in the majority of cases, unintentional or that it happens truly against the will of the parents and physicians. They say that it is a question of risks which are not all that different from those in natural procreation; to seek to generate new life without running any risks would in practice mean doing nothing to transmit it. It is true that not all the losses of embryos in the process of *in vitro* fertilization have the same relationship to the will of those involved in the procedure. But it is also true that in many cases the abandonment, destruction and loss of embryos are foreseen and willed.

---

27 Currently the number of embryos sacrificed, even in the most technically advanced centers of artificial fertilization, hovers above 80%.

Embryos produced *in vitro* which have defects are directly discarded. Cases are becoming ever more prevalent in which couples who have no fertility problems are using artificial means of procreation in order to engage in genetic selection of their offspring. In many countries, it is now common to stimulate ovulation so as to obtain a large number of oocytes which are then fertilized. Of these, some are transferred into the woman's uterus, while the others are frozen for future use. The reason for multiple transfer is to increase the probability that at least one embryo will implant in the uterus. In this technique, therefore, the number of embryos transferred is greater than the single child desired, in the expectation that some embryos will be lost and multiple pregnancy may not occur. In this way, the practice of multiple embryo transfer implies *a purely utilitarian treatment of embryos.* One is struck by the fact that, in any other area of medicine, ordinary professional ethics and the healthcare authorities themselves would never allow a medical procedure which involved such a high number of failures and fatalities. In fact, techniques of *in vitro* fertilization are accepted based on the presupposition that the individual embryo is not deserving of full respect in the presence of the competing desire for offspring which must be satisfied.

This sad reality, which often goes unmentioned, is truly deplorable: the "various techniques of artificial reproduction, which would seem to be at the service of life and which are frequently used with this intention, actually open the door to new threats against life."[28]

---

28 JOHN PAUL II, Encyclical Letter *Evangelium Vitae*, 14: AAS 87 (1995), 416.

16. The Church moreover holds that it is ethically unacceptable to *dissociate procreation from the integrally personal context of the conjugal act:*[29] human procreation is a personal act of a husband and wife, which is not capable of substitution. The blithe acceptance of the enormous number of abortions involved in the process of *in vitro* fertilization vividly illustrates how the replacement of the conjugal act by a technical procedure—in addition to being in contradiction with the respect that is due to procreation as something that cannot be reduced to mere reproduction—leads to a weakening of the respect owed to every human being. Recognition of such respect is, on the other hand, promoted by the intimacy of husband and wife nourished by married love.

The Church recognizes the legitimacy of the desire for a child and understands the suffering of couples struggling with problems of fertility. Such a desire, however, should not override the dignity of every human life to the point of absolute supremacy. The desire for a child cannot justify the "production" of offspring, just as the desire not to have a child cannot justify the abandonment or destruction of a child once he or she has been conceived.

In reality, it seems that some researchers, lacking any ethical point of reference and aware of the possibilities inherent in technological progress, surrender to the logic of

---

29   Cf. Pius XII, Address to the Second World Congress in Naples on human reproduction and sterility (19 May 1956): AAS 48 (1956), 470; Paul VI, Encyclical Letter *Humanae Vitae*, 12: AAS 60 (1968), 488-489; Congregation for the Doctrine of the Faith, Instruction *Donum Vitae*, II, B, 4-5: AAS 80 (1988), 90-94.

purely subjective desires[30] and to economic pressures which are so strong in this area. In the face of this manipulation of the human being in his or her embryonic state, it needs to be repeated that "God's love does not differentiate between the newly conceived infant still in his or her mother's womb and the child or young person, or the adult and the elderly person. God does not distinguish between them because he sees an impression of his own image and likeness (Gn 1:26) in each one. . . . Therefore, the Magisterium of the Church has constantly proclaimed the sacred and inviolable character of every human life from its conception until its natural end."[31]

Intracytoplasmic Sperm Injection (ICSI)

17. Among the recent techniques of artificial fertilization which have gradually assumed a particular importance is *intracytoplasmic sperm injection*.[32] This technique is used with

---

30 An increasing number of persons, even those who are unmarried, are having recourse to techniques of artificial reproduction in order to have a child. These actions weaken the institution of marriage and cause babies to be born in environments which are not conducive to their full human development.

31 BENEDICT XVI, Address to the General Assembly of the Pontifical Academy for Life and International Congress on "The Human Embryo in the Pre-implantation Phase" (27 February 2006): *AAS* 98 (2006), 264.

32 *Intracytoplasmic sperm injection* is similar in almost every respect to other forms of *in vitro* fertilization with the difference that in this procedure fertilization in the test tube does not take place on its own, but rather by means of the injection into the oocyte of a single sperm, selected earlier, or by the injection of immature germ cells taken from the man.

increasing frequency given its effectiveness in overcoming various forms of male infertility.[33]

Just as in general with *in vitro* fertilization, of which it is a variety, ICSI is intrinsically illicit: it causes *a complete separation between procreation and the conjugal act.* Indeed ICSI takes place "outside the bodies of the couple through actions of third parties whose competence and technical activity determine the success of the procedure. Such fertilization entrusts the life and identity of the embryo into the power of doctors and biologists and establishes the domination of technology over the origin and destiny of the human person. Such a relationship of domination is in itself contrary to the dignity and equality that must be common to parents and children. Conception *in vitro* is the result of the technical action which presides over fertilization. Such fertilization is neither in fact achieved nor positively willed as the expression and fruit of a specific act of the conjugal union."[34]

Freezing Embryos

18. One of the methods for improving the chances of success in techniques of *in vitro* fertilization is the multiplication of attempts. In order to avoid repeatedly taking oocytes from the woman's body, the process involves a single intervention in which multiple oocytes are taken, followed by cryopreservation of a considerable number of the embryos

---

33 There is ongoing discussion among specialists regarding the health risks which this method may pose for children conceived in this way.

34 CONGREGATION FOR THE DOCTRINE OF THE FAITH, Instruction *Donum Vitae*, II, B, 5: AAS 80 (1988), 93.

conceived *in vitro*.[35] In this way, should the initial attempt at achieving pregnancy not succeed, the procedure can be repeated or additional pregnancies attempted at a later date. In some cases, even the embryos used in the first transfer are frozen because the hormonal ovarian stimulation used to obtain the oocytes has certain effects which lead physicians to wait until the woman's physiological conditions have returned to normal before attempting to transfer an embryo into her womb.

Cryopreservation is *incompatible with the respect owed to human embryos*; it presupposes their production *in vitro*; it exposes them to the serious risk of death or physical harm, since a high percentage does not survive the process of freezing and thawing; it deprives them at least temporarily of maternal reception and gestation; it places them in a situation in which they are susceptible to further offense and manipulation.[36]

The majority of embryos that are not used remain "orphans." Their parents do not ask for them and at times all trace of the parents is lost. This is why there are thousands upon thousands of frozen embryos in almost all countries where *in vitro* fertilization takes place.

19. With regard to the large number of *frozen embryos already in existence* the question becomes: what to do with them? Some of those who pose this question do not grasp its ethical nature, motivated as they are by laws in some countries that require cryopreservation centers to empty their stor-

---

35 Cryopreservation of embryos refers to freezing them at extremely low temperatures, allowing long term storage.

36 Cf. CONGREGATION FOR THE DOCTRINE OF THE FAITH, Instruction *Donum Vitae*, I, 6: AAS 80 (1988), 84-85.

age tanks periodically. Others, however, are aware that a grave injustice has been perpetrated and wonder how best to respond to the duty of resolving it.

Proposals to *use these embryos for research* or *for the treatment of disease* are obviously unacceptable because they treat the embryos as mere "biological material" and result in their destruction. The proposal to thaw such embryos without reactivating them and use them for research, as if they were normal cadavers, is also unacceptable.[37]

The proposal that these embryos could be put at the disposal of infertile couples as a *treatment for infertility* is not ethically acceptable for the same reasons which make artificial heterologous procreation illicit as well as any form of surrogate motherhood;[38] this practice would also lead to other problems of a medical, psychological and legal nature.

It has also been proposed, solely in order to allow human beings to be born who are otherwise condemned to destruction, that there could be a form of "*prenatal adoption.*" This proposal, praiseworthy with regard to the intention of respecting and defending human life, presents however various problems not dissimilar to those mentioned above.

All things considered, it needs to be recognized that the thousands of abandoned embryos represent a *situation of injustice which in fact cannot be resolved.* Therefore John Paul II made an "appeal to the conscience of the world's scientific authorities and in particular to doctors, that the production of human embryos be halted, taking into account that there seems to be no morally licit solution regarding the human

---

37 Cf. numbers 34-35 below.

38 Cf. CONGREGATION FOR THE DOCTRINE OF THE FAITH, Instruction *Donum Vitae*, II, A, 1-3: AAS 80 (1988), 87-89.

destiny of the thousands and thousands of 'frozen' embryos which are and remain the subjects of essential rights and should therefore be protected by law as human persons."[39]

The Freezing of Oocytes

20. In order to avoid the serious ethical problems posed by the freezing of embryos, the freezing of oocytes has also been advanced in the area of techniques of *in vitro* fertilization.[40] Once a sufficient number of oocytes has been obtained for a series of attempts at artificial procreation, only those which are to be transferred into the mother's body are fertilized while the others are frozen for future fertilization and transfer should the initial attempts not succeed.

In this regard it needs to be stated that *cryopreservation of oocytes for the purpose of being used in artificial procreation is to be considered morally unacceptable.*

The Reduction of Embryos

21. Some techniques used in artificial procreation, above all the transfer of multiple embryos into the mother's womb, have caused a significant increase in the frequency of multiple pregnancy. This situation gives rise in turn to the practice of so-called embryo reduction, a procedure in which

---

39 JOHN PAUL II, Address to the participants in the Symposium on "*Evangelium Vitae* and Law" and the Eleventh International Colloquium on Roman and Canon Law (24 May 1996), 6: AAS 88 (1996), 943-944.

40 Cryopreservation of oocytes is also indicated in other medical contexts which are not under consideration here. The term oocyte refers to the female germ cell (gametocyte) not penetrated by the spermatozoa.

embryos or fetuses in the womb are directly exterminated. The decision to eliminate human lives, given that it was a human life that was desired in the first place, represents a contradiction that can often lead to suffering and feelings of guilt lasting for years.

From the ethical point of view, *embryo reduction is an intentional selective abortion.* It is in fact the deliberate and direct elimination of one or more innocent human beings in the initial phase of their existence and as such it always constitutes a grave moral disorder.[41]

The ethical justifications proposed for embryo reduction are often based on analogies with natural disasters or emergency situations in which, despite the best intentions of all involved, it is not possible to save everyone. Such analogies cannot in any way be the basis for an action which is directly abortive. At other times, moral principles are invoked, such as those of the lesser evil or double effect, which are likewise inapplicable in this case. It is never permitted to do something which is intrinsically illicit, not even in view of a good result: *the end does not justify the means.*

Preimplantation Diagnosis

22. Preimplantation diagnosis is a form of prenatal diagnosis connected with techniques of artificial fertilization in which embryos formed *in vitro* undergo genetic diagnosis before being transferred into a woman's womb. Such diagnosis is done *in order to ensure that only embryos free from*

---

41 Cf. SECOND VATICAN COUNCIL, Pastoral Constitution *Gaudium et Spes*, n. 51; JOHN PAUL II, Encyclical Letter *Evangelium Vitae*, 62: AAS 87 (1995), 472.

defects or having the desired sex or other particular qualities are transferred.

Unlike other forms of prenatal diagnosis, in which the diagnostic phase is clearly separated from any possible later elimination and which provide therefore a period in which a couple would be free to accept a child with medical problems, in this case, the diagnosis before implantation is immediately followed by the elimination of an embryo suspected of having genetic or chromosomal defects, or not having the sex desired, or having other qualities that are not wanted. Preimplantation diagnosis—connected as it is with artificial fertilization, which is itself always intrinsically illicit—is directed toward the *qualitative selection and consequent destruction of embryos*, which constitutes an act of abortion. Preimplantation diagnosis is therefore the expression of a *eugenic mentality* that "accepts selective abortion in order to prevent the birth of children affected by various types of anomalies. Such an attitude is shameful and utterly reprehensible, since it presumes to measure the value of a human life only within the parameters of 'normality' and physical well-being, thus opening the way to legitimizing infanticide and euthanasia as well."[42]

By treating the human embryo as mere "laboratory material," *the concept itself of human dignity is also subjected to alteration and discrimination.* Dignity belongs equally to every single human being, irrespective of his parents' desires, his social condition, educational formation or level of physical development. If at other times in history, while the concept and requirements of human dignity were accepted in general, discrimination was practiced on the basis of race,

---

42 John Paul II, Encyclical Letter *Evangelium Vitae*, 63: AAS 87 (1995), 473.

religion or social condition, today there is a no less serious and unjust form of discrimination which leads to the non-recognition of the ethical and legal status of human beings suffering from serious diseases or disabilities. It is forgotten that sick and disabled people are not some separate category of humanity; in fact, sickness and disability are part of the human condition and affect every individual, even when there is no direct experience of it. Such discrimination is immoral and must therefore be considered legally unacceptable, just as there is a duty to eliminate cultural, economic and social barriers which undermine the full recognition and protection of disabled or ill people.

New Forms of Interception and Contragestation

23. Alongside methods of preventing pregnancy which are, properly speaking, contraceptive, that is, which prevent conception following from a sexual act, there are other technical means which act after fertilization, when the embryo is already constituted, either before or after implantation in the uterine wall. Such methods are *interceptive* if they interfere with the embryo before implantation and *contragestative* if they cause the elimination of the embryo once implanted.

In order to promote wider use of interceptive methods,[43] it is sometimes stated that the way in which they function is not sufficiently understood. It is true that there is not always complete knowledge of the way that different pharmaceuticals operate, but scientific studies indicate that *the effect of inhibiting implantation is certainly present*, even if this does not mean that such interceptives cause an abortion every time

---

43 The interceptive methods which are best known are the IUD (intrauterine device) and the so-called "morning-after pills."

they are used, also because conception does not occur after every act of sexual intercourse. It must be noted, however, that anyone who seeks to prevent the implantation of an embryo which may possibly have been conceived, and who therefore either requests or prescribes such a pharmaceutical, generally intends abortion.

When there is a delay in menstruation, a contragestative is used,[44] usually one or two weeks after the non-occurrence of the monthly period. The stated aim is to re-establish menstruation, but what takes place in reality is the *abortion of an embryo which has just implanted.*

As is known, abortion is "the deliberate and direct killing, by whatever means it is carried out, of a human being in the initial phase of his or her existence, extending from conception to birth."[45] Therefore, the use of means of interception and contragestation fall within the *sin of abortion* and are gravely immoral. Furthermore, when there is certainty that an abortion has resulted, there are serious penalties in canon law.[46]

---

44 The principal means of contragestation are RU-486 (Mifepristone), synthetic prostaglandins or Methotrexate.

45 JOHN PAUL II, Encyclical Letter *Evangelium Vitae*, 58: AAS 87 (1995), 467.

46 Cf. CIC, can. 1398 and CCEO, can. 1450 § 2; cf. also CIC, can. 1323-1324. The Pontifical Commission for the Authentic Interpretation of the Code of Canon Law declared that the canonical concept of abortion is "the killing of the fetus in whatever way or at whatever time from the moment of conception" (*Response* of 23 May 1988: AAS 80 [1988], 1818).

Third Part:
New Treatments Which Involve the Manipulation of the Embryo or the Human Genetic Patrimony

24. Knowledge acquired in recent years has opened new perspectives for both regenerative medicine and for the treatment of genetically based diseases. In particular, *research on embryonic stem cells* and its possible future uses have prompted great interest, even though up to now such research has not produced effective results, as distinct from *research on adult stem cells*. Because some maintain that the possible medical advances which might result from research on embryonic stem cells could justify various forms of manipulation and destruction of human embryos, a whole range of questions has emerged in the area of gene therapy, from cloning to the use of stem cells, which call for attentive moral discernment.

Gene Therapy

25. *Gene therapy* commonly refers to techniques of genetic engineering applied to human beings for therapeutic purposes, that is to say, with the aim of curing genetically based diseases, although recently gene therapy has been attempted for diseases which are not inherited, for cancer in particular.

In theory, it is possible to use gene therapy on two levels: somatic cell gene therapy and germ line cell therapy. *Somatic cell gene therapy* seeks to eliminate or reduce genetic defects on the level of somatic cells, that is, cells other than the reproductive cells, but which make up the tissue and organs of the body. It involves procedures aimed at certain individual cells with effects that are limited to a single person. *Germ line cell therapy* aims instead at correcting genetic defects present in germ line cells with the purpose of transmitting the therapeutic effects to the offspring of the individual. Such methods of gene therapy, whether somatic or germ line cell therapy, can be undertaken on a fetus *before his or her birth* as gene therapy in the uterus or *after birth* on a child or adult.

26. For a moral evaluation the following distinctions need to be kept in mind. *Procedures used on somatic cells for strictly therapeutic purposes are in principle morally licit.* Such actions seek to restore the normal genetic configuration of the patient or to counter damage caused by genetic anomalies or those related to other pathologies. Given that gene therapy can involve significant risks for the patient, the ethical principle must be observed according to which, in order to proceed to a therapeutic intervention, it is necessary to establish beforehand that the person being treated will not be exposed to risks to his health or physical integrity which are excessive or disproportionate to the gravity of the pathology for which a cure is sought. The informed consent of the patient or his legitimate representative is also required.

The moral evaluation of *germ line cell therapy* is different. Whatever genetic modifications are effected on the germ cells of a person will be transmitted to any potential offspring. Because the risks connected to any genetic manipulation are considerable and as yet not fully controllable, *in the present state of research, it is not morally permissible to act in a way that may cause possible harm to the resulting progeny.* In the hypothesis of gene therapy on the embryo, it needs to be added that this only takes place in the context of *in vitro* fertilization and thus runs up against all the ethical objections to such procedures. For these reasons, therefore, it must be stated that, in its current state, germ line cell therapy in all its forms is morally illicit.

27. *The question of using genetic engineering for purposes other than medical treatment also calls for consideration.* Some have imagined the possibility of using techniques of genetic engineering to introduce alterations with the presumed aim of improving and strengthening the gene pool. Some of these proposals exhibit a certain dissatisfaction or even rejection of the value of the human being as a finite creature and person. Apart from technical difficulties and the real and potential risks involved, such manipulation would promote a eugenic mentality and would lead to indirect social stigma with regard to people who lack certain qualities, while privileging qualities that happen to be appreciated by a certain culture or society; such qualities do not constitute what is specifically human. This would be in contrast with the fundamental truth of the equality of all human beings which is expressed in the principle of justice, the violation of which, in the long run, would harm peaceful coexistence among individuals. Furthermore, one wonders who would be able to establish which modifications were to be held as positive and which not, or what limits should be placed on individual requests for improvement since it would be materially impossible to fulfil the wishes of every single person. Any conceivable response to these questions would, however, derive from arbitrary and questionable criteria. All of this leads to the conclusion that the prospect of such an intervention would end sooner or later by harming the common good, by favoring the will of some over the freedom of

others. Finally it must also be noted that in the attempt to create *a new type of human being* one can recognize *an ideological element* in which man tries to take the place of his Creator.

In stating the ethical negativity of these kinds of interventions which imply *an unjust domination of man over man*, the Church also recalls the need to return to an attitude of care for people and of education in accepting human life in its concrete historical finite nature.

Human Cloning

28. Human cloning refers to the asexual or agametic reproduction of the entire human organism in order to produce one or more "copies" which, from a genetic perspective, are substantially identical to the single original.[47]

Cloning is proposed for two basic purposes: *reproduction*, that is, in order to obtain the birth of a baby, and *medical therapy* or research. In theory, reproductive cloning would be able to satisfy certain specific desires, for example, control over human evolution, selection of human beings with superior qualities, pre-selection of the sex of a child to be born, production of a child who is the "copy" of another, or production of a child for a couple whose infertility cannot be

---

47 In the current state of knowledge, the techniques which have been proposed for accomplishing human cloning are two: artificial embryo twinning and cell nuclear transfer. *Artificial embryo twinning* consists in the artificial separation of individual cells or groups of cells from the embryo in the earliest stage of development. These are then transferred into the uterus in order to obtain identical embryos in an artificial manner. *Cell nuclear transfer*, or cloning properly speaking, consists in introducing a nucleus taken from an embryonic or somatic cell into an denucleated oocyte. This is followed by stimulation of the oocyte so that it begins to develop as an embryo.

treated in another way. Therapeutic cloning, on the other hand, has been proposed as a way of producing embryonic stem cells with a predetermined genetic patrimony in order to overcome the problem of immune system rejection; this is therefore linked to the issue of the use of stem cells.

Attempts at cloning have given rise to genuine concern throughout the entire world. Various national and international organizations have expressed negative judgments on human cloning and it has been prohibited in the great majority of nations.

Human cloning is intrinsically illicit in that, by taking the ethical negativity of techniques of artificial fertilization to their extreme, it seeks to *give rise to a new human being without a connection to the act of reciprocal self-giving between the spouses* and, more radically, *without any link to sexuality*. This leads to manipulation and abuses gravely injurious to human dignity.[48]

29. If cloning were to be done for *reproduction*, this would impose on the resulting individual a predetermined genetic identity, subjecting him—as has been stated—to a form of *biological slavery*, from which it would be difficult to free himself. The fact that someone would arrogate to himself the right to determine arbitrarily the genetic characteristics of another person represents *a grave offense to the dignity of that person as well as to the fundamental equality of all people*.

The originality of every person is a consequence of the particular relationship that exists between God and a human being from the first moment of his existence and carries with

---

48 Cf. CONGREGATION FOR THE DOCTRINE OF THE FAITH, Instruction *Donum Vitae*, I, 6: AAS 80 (1988), 84; JOHN PAUL II, Address to Members of the Diplomatic Corps accredited to the Holy See (10 January 2005), 5: AAS 97 (2005), 153.

it the obligation to respect the singularity and integrity of each person, even on the biological and genetic levels. In the encounter with another person, we meet a human being who owes his existence and his proper characteristics to the love of God, and only the love of husband and wife constitutes a mediation of that love in conformity with the plan of the Creator and heavenly Father.

30. From the ethical point of view, so-called therapeutic cloning is even more serious. To create embryos with the intention of destroying them, even with the intention of helping the sick, is completely incompatible with human dignity, because it makes the existence of a human being at the embryonic stage nothing more than a means to be used and destroyed. It is *gravely immoral to sacrifice a human life for therapeutic ends.*

The ethical objections raised in many quarters to therapeutic cloning and to the use of human embryos formed *in vitro* have led some researchers to propose new techniques which are presented as capable of producing stem cells of an embryonic type without implying the destruction of true human embryos.[49] These proposals have been met with questions of both a scientific and an ethical nature regarding above all the ontological status of the "product" obtained in this way. Until these doubts have been clarified, the statement of the Encyclical *Evangelium Vitae* needs to be kept in mind: "what is at stake is so important that, from the standpoint of moral obligation, the mere probability that a human person is involved would suffice to justify an abso-

---

49   The new techniques of this kind are, for example, the use of human parthenogenesis, altered nuclear transfer (ANT) and oocyte assisted reprogramming (OAR).

lutely clear prohibition of any intervention aimed at killing a human embryo."[50]

The Therapeutic Use of Stem Cells

31. Stem cells are undifferentiated cells with two basic characteristics: (a) the prolonged capability of multiplying themselves while maintaining the undifferentiated state; (b) the capability of producing transitory progenitor cells from which fully differentiated cells descend, for example, nerve cells, muscle cells and blood cells.

Once it was experimentally verified that when stem cells are transplanted into damaged tissue they tend to promote cell growth and the regeneration of the tissue, new prospects opened for regenerative medicine, which have been the subject of great interest among researchers throughout the world.

Among the sources for human stem cells which have been identified thus far are: the embryo in the first stages of its existence, the fetus, blood from the umbilical cord and various tissues from adult humans (bone marrow, umbilical cord, brain, mesenchyme from various organs, etc.) and amniotic fluid. At the outset, studies focused on *embryonic stem cells*, because it was believed that only these had significant capabilities of multiplication and differentiation. Numerous studies, however, show that *adult stem cells* also have a certain versatility. Even if these cells do not seem to have the same capacity for renewal or the same plasticity as stem cells taken from embryos, advanced scientific studies and experimentation indicate that these cells give more

---

50 John Paul II, Encyclical Letter *Evangelium Vitae*, 60: AAS 87 (1995), 469.

positive results than embryonic stem cells. Therapeutic protocols in force today provide for the use of adult stem cells and many lines of research have been launched, opening new and promising possibilities.

32. With regard to the ethical evaluation, it is necessary to consider the *methods of obtaining stem cells* as well as *the risks connected with their clinical and experimental use.*

In these methods, the origin of the stem cells must be taken into consideration. Methods which do not cause serious harm to the subject from whom the stem cells are taken are to be considered licit. This is generally the case when tissues are taken from (a) an adult organism; (b) the blood of the umbilical cord at the time of birth; (c) fetuses who have died of natural causes. The obtaining of stem cells from a living human embryo, on the other hand, invariably causes the death of the embryo and is consequently gravely illicit: "research, in such cases, irrespective of efficacious therapeutic results, is not truly at the service of humanity. In fact, this research advances through the suppression of human lives that are equal in dignity to the lives of other human individuals and to the lives of the researchers themselves. History itself has condemned such a science in the past and will condemn it in the future, not only because it lacks the light of God but also because it lacks humanity."[51]

The use of embryonic stem cells or differentiated cells derived from them—even when these are provided by other researchers through the destruction of embryos or

---

51 BENEDICT XVI, Address to the participants in the Symposium on the topic: "Stem Cells: what future for therapy?" organized by the Pontifical Academy for Life (16 September 2006): *AAS* 98 (2006), 694.

when such cells are commercially available—presents serious problems from the standpoint of cooperation in evil and scandal.[52]

There are no moral objections to the clinical use of stem cells that have been obtained licitly; however, the common criteria of medical ethics need to be respected. Such use should be characterized by scientific rigor and prudence, by reducing to the bare minimum any risks to the patient and by facilitating the interchange of information among clinicians and full disclosure to the public at large.

Research initiatives involving the use of adult stem cells, since they do not present ethical problems, should be encouraged and supported.[53]

Attempts at Hybridization

33. Recently animal oocytes have been used for reprogramming the nuclei of human somatic cells—this is generally called *hybrid cloning*—in order to extract embryonic stem cells from the resulting embryos without having to use human oocytes.

From the ethical standpoint, such procedures represent an offense against the dignity of human beings on account of *the admixture of human and animal genetic elements capable of disrupting the specific identity of man.* The possible use of the stem cells, taken from these embryos, may also involve additional health risks, as yet unknown, due to the presence of animal genetic

---

52   Cf. numbers 34-35 below.

53   Cf. BENEDICT XVI, Address to the participants in the Symposium on the topic: "Stem Cells: what future for therapy?" organized by the Pontifical Academy for Life (16 September 2006): AAS 98 (2006), 693-695.

material in their cytoplasm. To consciously expose a human being to such risks is morally and ethically unacceptable.

The Use of Human "Biological Material" of Illicit Origin

34. For scientific research and for the production of vaccines or other products, cell lines are at times used which are the result of an illicit intervention against the life or physical integrity of a human being. The connection to the unjust act may be either mediate or immediate, since it is generally a question of cells which reproduce easily and abundantly. This "material" is sometimes made available commercially or distributed freely to research centers by governmental agencies having this function under the law. All of this gives rise to various ethical problems with regard to cooperation in evil and with regard to scandal. It is fitting therefore to formulate general principles on the basis of which people of good conscience can evaluate and resolve situations in which they may possibly be involved on account of their professional activity.

It needs to be remembered above all that the category of abortion "is to be applied also to the recent forms of *intervention on human embryos* which, although carried out for purposes legitimate in themselves, inevitably involve the killing of those embryos. This is the case with *experimentation on embryos*, which is becoming increasingly widespread in the field of biomedical research and is legally permitted in some countries . . . [T]he use of human embryos or fetuses as an object of experimentation constitutes a crime against their dignity as human beings who have a right to the same respect owed to a child once born, just as to every person."[54] These forms of experimentation always constitute a grave moral disorder.[55]

35. A different situation is created when researchers use "biological material" of illicit origin which has been produced apart from their research center or which has been obtained commercially. The Instruction *Donum Vitae* formulated the general principle which must be observed in these cases: "The corpses of human embryos and fetuses, whether they have been deliberately aborted or not, must be respected just as the remains of other human beings. In particular, they cannot be subjected to mutilation or to autopsies if their death has not yet been verified and without the consent of the parents or of the mother. Furthermore, the moral requirements must be safeguarded that there be no complicity in deliberate abortion and that the risk of scandal be avoided."[56]

In this regard, *the criterion of independence as it has been formulated by some ethics committees is not sufficient*. According to this criterion, the use of "biological material" of illicit origin would be ethically permissible provided there is a clear separation between those who, on the one hand, produce, freeze and cause the death of embryos and, on the other, the researchers involved in scientific experimentation. The criterion of independence is not sufficient to avoid a

---

54 JOHN PAUL II, Encyclical Letter *Evangelium Vitae*, 63: AAS 87 (1995), 472-473.

55 Cf. JOHN PAUL II, Encyclical Letter *Evangelium Vitae*, 62: AAS 87 (1995), 472.

56 CONGREGATION FOR THE DOCTRINE OF THE FAITH, Instruction *Donum Vitae*, I, 4: AAS 80 (1988), 83.

contradiction in the attitude of the person who says that he does not approve of the injustice perpetrated by others, but at the same time accepts for his own work the "biological material" which the others have obtained by means of that injustice. When the illicit action is endorsed by the laws which regulate healthcare and scientific research, it is necessary to distance oneself from the evil aspects of that system in order not to give the impression of a certain toleration or tacit acceptance of actions which are gravely unjust.[57] Any appearance of acceptance would in fact contribute to the growing indifference to, if not the approval of, such actions in certain medical and political circles.

At times, the objection is raised that the above-mentioned considerations would mean that people of good conscience involved in research would have the duty to oppose actively all the illicit actions that take place in the field of medicine, thus excessively broadening their ethical responsibility. In reality, the duty to avoid cooperation in evil and scandal relates to their ordinary professional activities, which they must pursue in a just manner and by means of which they must give witness to the value of life by their opposition to gravely unjust laws. Therefore, it needs to be stated that there is a duty to refuse to use such "biological material" even when there is no close connection between the researcher and the actions of those who performed the artificial fertilization or the abortion, or when there was

---

57 Cf. JOHN PAUL II, Encyclical Letter *Evangelium Vitae*, 73: *AAS* 87 (1995), 486: "Abortion and euthanasia are thus crimes which no human law can claim to legitimize. There is no obligation in conscience to obey such laws; instead there is a *grave and clear obligation to oppose them by conscientious objection.*" The right of conscientious objection, as an expression of the right to freedom of conscience, should be protected by law.

no prior agreement with the centers in which the artificial fertilization took place. This duty springs from the necessity to *remove oneself*, within the area of one's own research, *from a gravely unjust legal situation and to affirm with clarity the value of human life*. Therefore, the above-mentioned criterion of independence is necessary, but may be ethically insufficient.

Of course, within this general picture there exist *differing degrees of responsibility*. Grave reasons may be morally proportionate to justify the use of such "biological material." Thus, for example, danger to the health of children could permit parents to use a vaccine which was developed using cell lines of illicit origin, while keeping in mind that everyone has the duty to make known their disagreement and to ask that their healthcare system make other types of vaccines available. Moreover, in organizations where cell lines of illicit origin are being utilized, the responsibility of those who make the decision to use them is not the same as that of those who have no voice in such a decision.

In the context of the urgent need to *mobilize consciences in favor of life*, people in the field of healthcare need to be reminded that "their responsibility today is greatly increased. Its deepest inspiration and strongest support lie in the intrinsic and undeniable ethical dimension of the health-care profession, something already recognized by the ancient and still relevant *Hippocratic Oath*, which requires every doctor to commit himself to absolute respect for human life and its sacredness."[58]

---

58 JOHN PAUL II, Encyclical Letter *Evangelium Vitae*, 63: AAS 89 (1995), 502.

Conclusion

36. There are those who say that the moral teaching of the Church contains too many prohibitions. In reality, however, her teaching is based on the recognition and promotion of all the gifts which the Creator has bestowed on man: such as life, knowledge, freedom and love. Particular appreciation is due not only to man's intellectual activities, but also to those which are practical, like work and technological activities. By these, in fact, he participates in the creative power of God and is called to transform creation by ordering its many resources toward the dignity and wellbeing of all human beings and of the human person in his entirety. In this way, man acts as the steward of the value and intrinsic beauty of creation.

Human history shows, however, how man has abused and can continue to abuse the power and capabilities which God has entrusted to him, giving rise to *various forms of unjust discrimination and oppression* of the weakest and most defenseless: the daily attacks on human life; the existence of large regions of poverty where people are dying from hunger and disease, excluded from the intellectual and practical resources available in abundance in many countries; technological and industrial development which is creating the real risk of a collapse of the ecosystem; the use of scientific research in the areas of physics, chemistry and biology for purposes of waging war; the many conflicts which still divide peoples and cultures; these sadly are only some of the most obvious signs of how man can make bad use of his abilities and become his own worst enemy by losing the awareness of his lofty and specific vocation to collaborate in the creative work of God.

At the same time, human history has also shown real *progress in the understanding and recognition of the value and dignity of every person* as the foundation of the rights and ethical imperatives by which human society has been, and continues to be structured. Precisely in the name of promoting human dignity, therefore, practices and forms of behavior harmful to that dignity have been prohibited. Thus, for example, there are legal and political—and not just ethical—prohibitions of racism, slavery, unjust discrimination and marginalization of women, children, and ill and disabled people. Such prohibitions bear witness to the inalienable value and intrinsic dignity of every human being and are a sign of genuine progress in human history. In other words, the legitimacy of every prohibition is based on the need to protect an authentic moral good.

37. If initially human and social progress was characterized primarily by industrial development and the production of consumer goods, today it is distinguished by developments in information technologies, research in genetics, medicine and biotechnologies for human benefit, which are areas of great importance for the future of humanity, but in which there are also evident and unacceptable abuses. "Just as a century ago it was the working classes which were oppressed in their fundamental rights, and the Church courageously came to their defense by proclaiming the sacrosanct rights of the worker as person, so now, when another category of persons is being oppressed in the fundamental right to life, the Church feels in duty bound to speak out with the same courage on behalf of those who have no voice. Hers is always the evangelical cry in defense of the world's poor,

those who are threatened and despised and whose human rights are violated."[59]

In virtue of the Church's doctrinal and pastoral mission, the Congregation for the Doctrine of the Faith has felt obliged to reiterate both the dignity and the fundamental and inalienable rights of every human being, including those in the initial stages of their existence, and to state explicitly the need for protection and respect which this dignity requires of everyone.

The fulfillment of this duty implies courageous opposition to all those practices which result in grave and unjust discrimination against unborn human beings, who have the dignity of a person, created like others in the image of God. *Behind every "no" in the difficult task of discerning between good and evil, there shines a great "yes" to the recognition of the dignity and inalienable value of every single and unique human being called into existence.*

The Christian faithful will commit themselves to the energetic promotion of a new culture of life by receiving the contents of this Instruction with the religious assent of their spirit, knowing that God always gives the grace necessary to observe his commandments and that, in every human being, above all in the least among us, one meets Christ himself (cf. Mt 25:40). In addition, all persons of good will, in particular physicians and researchers open to dialogue and desirous of knowing what is true, will understand and agree with these principles and judgments, which seek to safeguard the vulnerable condition of human beings in the first stages of life and to promote a more human civilization.

---

59 JOHN PAUL II, Letter to all the Bishops on "The Gospel of Life" (19 May 1991): AAS 84 (1992), 319.

The Sovereign Pontiff Benedict XVI, in the Audience granted to the undersigned Cardinal Prefect on 20 June 2008, approved the present Instruction, adopted in the Ordinary Session of this Congregation, and ordered its publication.

Rome, from the Offices of the Congregation for the Doctrine of the Faith, 8 September 2008, Feast of the Nativity of the Blessed Virgin Mary.

Cardinal William Levada
Prefect

+ Luis F. Ladaria, S.I.
Titular Archbishop of Thibica
Secretary

Part II

ADDITIONAL
RESOURCES

Summary of the Instruction *Dignitas Personae*

Vatican Press Office

Aim

In recent years, biomedical research has made great strides, opening new possibilities for the treatment of disease, but also giving rise to serious questions which had not been directly treated in the Instruction *Donum Vitae* (22 February 1987). A new Instruction, which is dated 8 September 2008, the Feast of the Nativity of the Blessed Virgin Mary, seeks to provide some responses to these new bioethical questions, as these have been the focus of expectations and concerns in large sectors of society. In this way, the Congregation for the Doctrine of the Faith seeks both to contribute "*to the formation of conscience*" (n. 10) and to encourage biomedical research respectful of the dignity of every human being and of procreation.

Title

The Instruction opens with the words *Dignitas personae*— the dignity of a person, which must be recognized in every human being from conception to natural death. This fundamental principle expresses "*a great 'yes' to human life* and must be at the center of ethical reflection on biomedical research" (n. 1).

Value

The document is an Instruction of a doctrinal nature, published by the Congregation for the Doctrine of the Faith and expressly approved by the Holy Father, Pope Benedict XVI. The Instruction therefore falls within the category of documents that "participate in the ordinary Magisterium of the successor of Peter" (Instruction *Donum Veritatis*, n. 18), and is to be received by Catholics "with the religious assent of their spirit" (*Dignitas Personae*, n. 37).

Preparation

For several years, the Congregation for the Doctrine of the Faith has been studying new biomedical questions with a view to updating the Instruction *Donum Vitae*. In undertaking the examination of such new questions, the Congregation for the Doctrine of the Faith "has benefited from the analysis of the Pontifical Academy for Life and has consulted numerous experts with regard to the scientific aspects of these questions, in order to address them with the principles of Christian anthropology. The Encyclicals *Veritatis Splendor* and *Evangelium Vitae* of John Paul II, as well as other interventions of the Magisterium, offer clear indications with regard to both the method and the content of the examination of the problems under consideration" (n. 2).

Intended recipients of the document

The Instruction is meant for "all who seek the truth" (n. 3). Indeed, in presenting principles and moral evaluations regarding biomedical research on human life, the Catholic Church "draws upon *the light both of reason and of faith* and seeks to set forth an integral vision of man and his vocation, capable of incorporating everything that is good in human activity, as well as in various cultural and religious traditions which not infrequently demonstrate a great reverence for life" (n. 3).

Structure
The Instruction has three parts: "the first recalls some anthropological, theological and ethical elements of fundamental importance; the second addresses new problems regarding procreation; the third examines new procedures involving the manipulation of embryos and the human genetic patrimony" (n. 3).

First Part: Anthropological, Theological and Ethical Aspects of Human Life and Procreation

The two fundamental principles

- "The human being is to be respected and treated as a person from the moment of conception; and therefore from that same moment his rights as a person must be recognized, among which in the first place is the inviolable right of every innocent human being to life" (n. 4).

- "The origin of human life has its authentic context in marriage and in the family, where it is generated through an act which expresses the reciprocal love between a man and a woman. Procreation which is truly responsible vis-à-vis the child to be born must be the fruit of marriage" (n. 6).

Faith and human dignity

"It is the Church's conviction that what is human is not only received and respected by *faith*, but is also purified, elevated and perfected" (n. 7). God has created every human being in his own image, and his Son has made it possible for us to become children of God. "By taking the interrelationship of these two dimensions, the human and the divine, as the starting point, one understands better why it is that man has unassailable value: he possesses an eternal vocation and is called to share in the trinitarian love of the living God" (n. 8.).

Faith and married life

"These two dimensions of life, the natural and the supernatural, allow us to understand better the sense in which the acts that permit a new human being to come into existence, in which a man and a woman give themselves to each other, are a reflection of trinitarian love. God, who is love and life, has inscribed in man and woman the vocation to share in a special way in his mystery of personal communion and in his work as Creator and Father . . . The Holy Spirit who is poured out in the sacramental celebration offers Christian couples the gift of a new communion of love that is the living and real image of that unique unity which makes of the Church the indivisible Mystical Body of the Lord Jesus" (n. 9).

The Church's Magisterium and the legitimate autonomy of science

"The Church, by expressing an ethical judgment on some developments of recent medical research concerning man and his beginnings, does not intervene in the area proper to medical science itself, but rather calls everyone to ethical and social responsibility for their actions. She reminds them that the ethical value of biomedical science is gauged in reference to both the unconditional respect owed to every human being at every moment of his or her existence, and the defense of the specific character of the personal act which transmits life" (n. 10).

Second Part: New Problems Concerning Procreation

Techniques for assisting fertility

Among the procedures which respond to problems of fertility are the following:

- "techniques of heterologous artificial fertilization" (n. 12): that is, "techniques used to obtain a human conception artificially by the use of gametes coming from at least one donor other than the spouses who are joined in marriage" (footnote 22).

- "techniques of homologous artificial fertilization" (n. 12): that is, "the technique used to obtain a human conception using the gametes of the two spouses joined in marriage" (footnote 23).

- "techniques which act as an aid to the conjugal act and its fertility" (n. 12).

- "techniques aimed at removing obstacles to natural fertilization" (n. 13).

- "adoption" (n. 13).

Techniques are morally permissible if they respect: "the right to life and to physical integrity of every human being," "the unity of marriage, which means reciprocal respect for the right within marriage to become a father or mother only together with the other spouse" and "the specifically human values of sexuality" (n. 12), which require that the procreation of a new human person come about as a result of the conjugal act specific to the love between a husband and wife.

- Therefore, "techniques which act as an aid to the conjugal act and its fertility are permitted" (n. 12). In such procedures, the "medical intervention respects the dignity of persons when it seeks to assist the conjugal act either in order to facilitate its performance or in order to enable it to achieve its objective once it has been normally performed" (n. 12).

- "Certainly, techniques aimed at removing obstacles to natural fertilization . . . are licit" (n. 13).

- "Adoption should be encouraged, promoted and facilitated so that the many children who lack parents may receive a home . . . In addition, research and investment directed at the prevention of sterility deserve encouragement (n. 13).

In vitro fertilization and the deliberate destruction of embryos

The experience of recent years has shown that in all techniques of *in vitro* fertilization "the number of embryos sacrificed is extremely high" (n. 14). Even in the most technically advanced centers of artificial fertilization, the number is above 80% (cf. footnote 27). "Embryos produced *in vitro* which have defects are directly discarded"; an increasing number of couples "are using artificial means of procreation in order to engage in genetic selection of their offspring"; of the embryos which are produced *in vitro* "some are transferred into the woman's uterus, while the others are frozen"; the technique of multiple transfer in which "the number of embryos transferred is greater than the single child desired, in the expectation that some embryos will be lost . . . implies a purely utilitarian treatment of embryos" (n. 15).

"The blithe acceptance of the enormous number of abortions involved in the process of *in vitro* fertilization vividly illustrates how the replacement of the conjugal act by a technical procedure . . . leads to a weakening of the respect owed to every human being. Recognition of such respect is, on the other hand, promoted by the intimacy of husband and wife nourished by married love . . . In the face of this manipulation of the human being in his or her embryonic state, it needs to be repeated that God's love does not differentiate between the newly conceived infant still in his or her mother's womb and the child or young person, or the adult and the elderly person. God does not distinguish between them because he sees an impression of his own image and likeness . . . Therefore, the Magisterium of the Church has constantly proclaimed the sacred and inviolable character of every human life from its conception until its natural end" (n. 16).

Intracytoplasmic sperm injection (ICSI)

Intracytoplasmic sperm injection is a variety of *in vitro* procreation in which fertilization in the test tube does not simply "take place on its own, but rather by means of the injection into the oocyte of a single sperm, selected earlier, or by the injection of immature germ cells taken from the man" (footnote 32).

This technique, which is morally illicit, causes a complete separation between procreation and the conjugal act" (n. 17). It takes place "outside the bodies of the couple through actions of third parties whose competence and technical activity determine the success of the procedure. Such fertilization entrusts the life and identity of the embryo into the power of doctors and biologists and establishes the domination of technology over the origin and destiny of the human person" (n. 17).

Freezing embryos

"In order to avoid repeatedly taking oocytes from the woman's body, the process involves a single intervention in which multiple oocytes are taken, followed by cryopreservation of a considerable number of the embryos conceived *in vitro*. In this way, should the initial attempt at achieving pregnancy not succeed, the procedure can be repeated or additional pregnancies attempted at a later date" (n. 18). The freezing or cryopreservation of embryos "refers to freezing them at extremely low temperatures, allowing long term storage" (cf. footnote 35).

"Cryopreservation is incompatible with the respect owed to human embryos; it presupposes their production *in vitro*; it exposes them to the serious risk of death or physical harm, since a high percentage does not survive the process of freezing and thawing; it deprives them at least temporarily of maternal reception and gestation; it places them in a situation in which they are susceptible to further offense and manipulation" (n. 18).

With regard to the large number of frozen embryos already in existence the question becomes: what to do with them? All the answers that have been proposed (use the embryos for research or for the treatment of disease; thaw them without reactivating them and use them for research, as if they were normal cadavers; put them at the disposal of infertile couples as a "treatment for infertility"; allow a form of "prenatal adoption") present real problems of various kinds. It needs to be recognized "that the thousands of abandoned embryos represent a situation of injustice which in fact cannot be resolved." Therefore, John Paul II made an "appeal to the conscience of the world's scientific authorities and in particular to doctors, that the production of human embryos be halted, taking into account that there seems to be no morally licit solution regarding the human destiny of the thousands and thousands of 'frozen' embryos which are and remain the subjects of essential rights and should therefore be protected by law as human persons" (n. 19).

The freezing of oocytes

"In order avoid the serious ethical problems posed by the freezing of embryos, the freezing of oocytes has also been advanced in the area of techniques of *in vitro* fertilization" (n. 20).

In this regard it needs to be stated that while the cryopreservation of oocytes is not in itself immoral, and is employed in other medical contexts which are not the subject of this document, when it takes place "for the purpose of being used in artificial procreation" it is "to be considered morally unacceptable" (n. 20).

The reduction of embryos

"Some techniques used in artificial procreation, above all the transfer of multiple embryos into the mother's womb, have caused a significant increase in the frequency of multiple pregnancy. This situation gives rise in turn to the practice of so-called embryo reduction, a procedure in which embryos or fetuses in the womb are directly exterminated" (n. 21).

"From the ethical point of view, embryo reduction is an intentional selective abortion. It is in fact the deliberate and direct elimination of one or more innocent human beings in the initial phase of their existence and as such it always constitutes a grave moral disorder" (n. 21).

Preimplantation diagnosis

"Preimplantation diagnosis is a form of prenatal diagnosis connected with techniques of artificial fertilization in which embryos formed *in vitro* undergo genetic diagnosis before being transferred into a woman's womb. Such diagnosis is done in order to ensure that only embryos free from defects or having the desired sex or other particular qualities are transferred" (n. 22).

"Unlike other forms of prenatal diagnosis . . . , diagnosis before implantation is immediately followed by the elimination of an embryo suspected of having genetic or chromosomal defects, or not having the sex desired, or having other qualities that are not wanted. Preimplantation diagnosis . . . is directed toward the qualitative selection and consequent destruction of embryos, which constitutes an act of abortion . . . By treating the human embryo as mere 'laboratory material,' the concept itself of human dignity is also subjected to alteration and discrimination . . . Such discrimination is immoral and must therefore be considered legally unacceptable . . ." (n. 22).

New forms of interception and contragestation
There are methods of preventing pregnancy which act after fertilization, when the embryo is already constituted.

- "Such methods are interceptive if they interfere with the embryo before implantation" (n. 23); for example, the IUD (intrauterine device) and the so-called 'morning-after pills' (footnote 42).

- They are "contragestative if they cause the elimination of the embryo once implanted" (n. 23); for example, the pharmaceutical known commercially as RU-486 (footnote 43).

Even if such interceptives may not cause an abortion every time they are used, also because conception does not occur after every act of sexual intercourse, it must be noted, however, that "anyone who seeks to prevent the implantation of an embryo which may possibly have been conceived and who therefore either requests or prescribes such a pharmaceutical, generally intends abortion." In the case of contragestatives "what takes place in reality is the abortion of an embryo which has just implanted . . . the use of means of interception and contragestation fall within the *sin of abortion* and are gravely immoral" (n. 23).

Third Part: New Treatments Which Involve the Manipulation of the Embryo or the Human Genetic Patrimony

Gene therapy
Gene therapy commonly refers to "techniques of genetic engineering applied to human beings for therapeutic purposes, that is to say, with the aim of curing genetically based diseases" (n. 25).

- Somatic cell gene therapy "seeks to eliminate or reduce genetic defects on the level of somatic cells" (n. 25).

- Germ line cell therapy aims "at correcting genetic defects present in germ line cells with the purpose of transmitting the therapeutic effects to the offspring of the individual" (n. 25).

From the ethical point of view:

- Procedures used on somatic cells for strictly therapeutic purposes "are in principle morally licit . . . Given that gene therapy can involve significant risks for the patient, the ethical principle must be observed according to which, in order to proceed to a therapeutic intervention, it is necessary to establish beforehand that the person being treated will not be exposed to risks to his health or physical integrity which are excessive or disproportionate to the gravity of the pathology for which a cure is sought. The informed consent of the patient or his legitimate representative is also required" (n. 26).

- With regard to germ line cell therapy, "the risks connected to any genetic manipulation are considerable and as yet not fully controllable" and therefore "in the present state of research, it is not morally permissible to act in a way that may cause possible harm to the resulting progeny" (n. 26).

- With regard to the possibility of using techniques of genetic engineering to introduce alterations with the presumed aim of improving and strengthening the gene pool, it must be observed that such interventions would promote a "eugenic mentality" and would introduce an "indirect social stigma with regard to people who lack certain qualities, while privileging qualities that happen to be appreciated by a certain culture or society; such qualities do not constitute what is specifically human. This would be in contrast with the fundamental truth of the equality of all human beings which is expressed in the principle of justice, the violation of which, in the long run, would harm peaceful coexistence among individuals . . . Finally it must also be noted that in the attempt to create a new type of human being one can recognize an ideological element in which man tries to take the place of his Creator" (n. 27).

Human cloning

Human cloning refers to "the asexual or agametic reproduction of the entire human organism in order to produce one or more 'copies' which, from a genetic perspective, are substantially identical to the single original" (n. 28). The techniques which have been proposed for accomplishing human cloning are artificial embryo twinning, which "consists in the artificial separation of individual cells or groups of cells from the embryo in the earliest stage of development . . . which are then transferred into the uterus in order to obtain identical embryos in an artificial manner" (footnote 47) and cell nuclear transfer, which "consists in introducing a nucleus taken from an embryonic or somatic cell into an denucleated oocyte. This is followed by stimulation of the oocyte so that it begins to develop as an embryo" (footnote 47). Cloning is proposed for two basic purposes: *reproduction*, that is, in order to obtain the birth of a baby, and *medical therapy* or research.

Human cloning is "intrinsically illicit in that . . . it seeks to give rise to a new human being without a connection to the act of reciprocal self-giving between the spouses and, more radically, without any link to sexuality. This leads to manipulation and abuses gravely injurious to human dignity" (n. 28).

- With regard to reproductive cloning, "this would impose on the resulting individual a predetermined genetic identity, subjecting him—as has been stated—to a form of biological slavery, from which it

62

would be difficult to free himself. The fact that someone would arrogate to himself the right to determine
arbitrarily the genetic characteristics of another person represents a grave offense to the dignity of that
person as well as to the fundamental equality of all
people . . . In the encounter with another person, we
meet a human being who owes his existence and his
proper characteristics to the love of God, and only
the love of husband and wife constitutes a mediation of that love in conformity with the plan of the
Creator and heavenly Father" (n. 29).

- With regard to cloning for medical therapy or
  research, it must be said that to "create embryos
  with the intention of destroying them, even with
  the intention of helping the sick, is completely
  incompatible with human dignity, because it makes
  the existence of a human being at the embryonic
  stage nothing more than a means to be used and
  destroyed. It is gravely immoral to sacrifice a human
  life for therapeutic ends" (n. 30).

- As an alternative to therapeutic cloning some
  researchers have proposed new techniques which are
  presented as capable of producing stem cells of an
  embryonic type without implying the destruction of
  true human embryos, for example, by altered nuclear
  transfer (ANT) or oocyte assisted reprogramming
  (OAR). Doubts still remain, however, "regarding
  the ontological status of the 'product' obtained in
  this way" (n. 30).

The therapeutic use of stem cells

"Stem cells are undifferentiated cells with two basic characteristics: (a) the prolonged capability of multiplying themselves while maintaining the undifferentiated state; (b) the capability of producing transitory progenitor cells from which fully differentiated cells descend, for example, nerve cells, muscle cells and blood cells. Once it was experimentally verified that when stem cells are transplanted into damaged tissue they tend to promote cell growth and the regeneration of the tissue, new prospects opened for regenerative medicine, which have been the subject of great interest among researchers throughout the world" (n. 31).

For the ethical evaluation, it is necessary above all to consider the methods of obtaining stem cells.

- "Methods which do not cause serious harm to the subject from whom the stem cells are taken are to be considered licit. This is generally the case when tissues are taken from: (a) an adult organism; (b) the blood of the umbilical cord at the time of birth; (c) fetuses who have died of natural causes" (n. 32).

- "The obtaining of stem cells from a living human embryo . . . invariably causes the death of the embryo and is consequently gravely illicit . . . In this case, research . . . is not truly at the service of humanity. In fact, this research advances through the suppression of human lives that are equal in dignity to the lives of other human individuals and to the lives of the researchers themselves" (n. 32).

- "The use of embryonic stem cells or differentiated cells derived from them—even when these are provided by other researchers through the destruction of embryos or when such cells are commercially available—presents serious problems from the standpoint of cooperation in evil and scandal" (n. 32).

Numerous studies, however, have shown that adult stem cells give more positive results than embryonic stem cells.

Attempts at hybridization

"Recently animal oocytes have been used for reprogramming the nuclei of human somatic cells . . . in order to extract embryonic stem cells from the resulting embryos without having to use human oocytes" (n. 33).

"From the ethical standpoint, such procedures represent an offense against the dignity of human beings on account of the admixture of human and animal genetic elements capable of disrupting the specific identity of man" (n. 33).

The use of human "biological material" of illicit origin

For scientific research and for the production of vaccines or other products, cell lines are at times used which are the result of an illicit intervention against the life or physical integrity of a human being.

- Experimentation on human embryos "constitutes a crime against their dignity as human beings who have a right to the same respect owed to a child once born, just as to every person. These forms of experimentation always constitute a grave moral disorder" (n. 34).

- With regard to the use of "biological material" of illicit origin by researchers, which has been produced apart from their research center or which has been obtained commercially, the moral requirement "must be safeguarded that there be no complicity in deliberate abortion and that the risk of scandal be avoided. In this regard, the criterion of independence as it has been formulated by some ethics committees is not sufficient. According to this criterion, the use of 'biological material' of illicit origin would be ethically permissible provided there is a clear separation between those who, on the one hand, produce, freeze and cause the death of embryos and, on the other, the researchers involved in scientific experimentation." It needs to be remembered that the "duty to refuse to use such 'biological material' springs from the necessity to remove oneself, within the area of one's own research, from a gravely unjust legal situation and to affirm with clarity the value of human life. Therefore, the above-mentioned criterion of independence is necessary, but may be ethically insufficient" (n. 35).

- "Of course, within this general picture there exist differing degrees of responsibility. Grave reasons may be morally proportionate to justify the use of such 'biological material.' Thus, for example, danger to the health of children could permit parents to use a vaccine which was developed using cell lines of illicit origin, while keeping in mind that everyone has the duty to make known their disagreement and to ask that their healthcare system make other types of vaccines available. Moreover, in organizations where cell lines of illicit origin are being utilized, the responsibility of those who make the decision to use them is not the same as that of those who have no voice in such a decision" (n. 35).

Address to the Symposium on the Theme "Stem Cells: What Future for Therapy?" Organized by the Pontifical Academy for Life

Pope Benedict XVI

Venerable Brothers in the Episcopate and in the Priesthood, Distinguished Ladies and Gentlemen,

I address a cordial greeting to you all. This meeting with you, scientists and scholars dedicated to specialized research in the treatment of diseases that are a serious affliction to humanity, is a special comfort to me.

I am grateful to the organizers who have promoted this Congress on a topic that has become more and more important in recent years. The specific theme of the Symposium is appropriately formulated with a question open to hope: *"Stem cells: what future for therapy?"*

I thank Bishop Elio Sgreccia, President of the Pontifical Academy for Life, for his kind words, also on behalf of the International Federation of Catholic Medical Associations (FIAMC), an association that has cooperated in organizing the Congress and is represented here by Prof. Gianluigi Gigli, outgoing President, and Prof. Simon de Castellvi, President-elect.

When science is applied to the alleviation of suffering and when it discovers on its way new resources, it shows two faces rich in humanity: through the sustained ingenuity invested in research, and through the benefit announced to all who are afflicted by sickness.

Those who provide financial means and encourage the necessary structures for study share in the merit of this progress on the path of civilization.

On this occasion, I would like to repeat what I said at a recent Audience: "Progress becomes true progress only if it serves the human person and if the human person grows: not only in terms of his or her technical power, but also in his or her moral awareness" (cf. General Audience, 16 August 2006).

In this light, somatic stem-cell research also deserves approval and encouragement when it felicitously combines scientific knowledge, the most advanced technology in the biological field and ethics that postulate respect for the human being at every stage of his or her existence.

The prospects opened by this new chapter in research are fascinating in themselves, for they give a glimpse of the possible cure of degenerative tissue diseases that subsequently threaten those affected with disability and death.

How is it possible not to feel the duty to praise all those who apply themselves to this research and all who support the organization and cover its expenses?

I would like in particular to urge scientific structures that draw their inspiration and organization from the Catholic Church to increase this type of research and to establish the closest possible contact with one another and with those who seek to relieve human suffering in the proper ways.

May I also point out, in the face of the frequently unjust accusations of insensitivity addressed to the Church, her constant support for research dedicated to the cure of diseases and to the good of humanity throughout her 2,000-year-old history.

If there has been resistance—and if there still is—it was and is to those forms of research that provide for the planned suppression of human beings who already exist, even if they have not yet been born. Research, in such cases, irrespective of efficacious therapeutic results is not truly at the service of humanity.

In fact, this research advances through the suppression of human lives that are equal in dignity to the lives of other human individuals and the lives of the researchers themselves.

History itself has condemned such a science in the past and will condemn it in the future, not only because it lacks the light of God but also because it lacks humanity.

I would like to repeat here what I already wrote some time ago: Here there is a problem that we cannot get around; no one can dispose of human life. An insurmountable limit to our possibilities of doing and of experimenting must be established. The human being is not a disposable object, but every single individual represents God's presence in the world (cf. J. Ratzinger, *God and the World*, Ignatius Press, 2002).

In the face of the actual suppression of the human being there can be no compromises or prevarications. One cannot think that a society can effectively combat crime when society itself legalizes crime in the area of conceived life.

On the occasion of recent Congresses of the Pontifical Academy for Life, I have had the opportunity to reassert the teaching of the Church, addressed to all people of good will, on the human value of the newly conceived child, also when considered prior to implantation in the uterus.

The fact that you at this Congress have expressed your commitment and hope to achieve new therapeutic results from the use of cells of the adult body without recourse to the suppression of newly conceived human beings, and the fact that your work is being rewarded by results, are confirmation of the validity of the Church's constant invitation to full respect for the human being from conception. The good of human beings should not only be sought in universally valid goals, but also in the methods used to achieve them.

A good result can never justify intrinsically unlawful means. It is not only a matter of a healthy criterion for the use of limited financial resources, but also, and above all, of respect for the fundamental human rights in the area of scientific research itself.

I hope that God will grant your efforts—which are certainly sustained by God who acts in every person of good will and for the good of all—the joy of discovering the truth, wisdom in consideration and respect for every human being, and success in the search for effective remedies to human suffering.

To seal this hope, I cordially impart an affectionate Blessing to all of you, to your collaborators and to your relatives, as well as to the patients who will benefit from your ingenuity and resourcefulness and the results of your work, with the assurance of my special remembrance in prayer.

Hall of the Swiss, Castel Gandolfo
Saturday, September 16, 2006

For Further Reading

Papal Documents

Pope Benedict XVI. Address to participants in the plenary session of the Congregation for the Doctrine of the Faith. January 31, 2008. *www.vatican.va/holy_father/benedict_xvi/ speeches/2008/january/documents/hf_ben-xvi_spe_20080131 _dottrina-fede_en.html*.

Pope Benedict XVI. Address to participants at the Twelfth General Assembly of the Pontifical Academy for Life and the Congress on the Human Embryo in the Pre-Implantation Phase. February 27, 2006. *www.vatican.va/holy_ father/benedict_xvi/speeches/2006/february/documents/hf_ben-xvi _spe_20060227_embrione-umano_en.html*.

Pope John Paul II. *The Gospel of Life (Evangelium Vitae)*. Washington, DC: USCCB, 1995. Also available at *www. vatican.va/holy_father/john_paul_ii/encyclicals/documents/ hf_jp-ii_enc_25031995_evangelium-vitae_en.html*.

Pope Paul VI. *On the Regulation of Birth (Humanae Vitae)*. Washington, DC: USCCB, 1968. Also available at *www. vatican.va/holy_father/paul_vi/encyclicals/documents/ hf_p-vi_enc_25071968_humanae-vitae_en.html*.

Curial Documents

Catechism of the Catholic Church (2nd ed.), no. 2323. Washington, DC: Libreria Editrice Vaticana–United States Conference of Catholic Bishops, 2001.

Congregation for the Doctrine of the Faith. *The Gift of Life (Donum Vitae): Instruction on Respect for Human Life in its Origin and on the Dignity of Procreation. www.vatican.va/ roman_curia/congregations/cfaith/documents/rc_con_cfaith_ doc_19870222_respect-for-human-life_en.html.*

Holy See Delegation to the UN. Intervention at the special committee of the Fifty-Seventh General Assembly of the UN on human embryonic cloning. September 23, 2002. *www.vatican.va/roman_curia/secretariat_state/documents/ rc_seg-st_doc_20020923_martino-cloning_en.html.*

Lopez Trujillo, Cardinal Alfonso. *Cloning: The Disappearance of Direct Parenthood and Denial of the Family. www.vatican.va/ roman_curia/pontifical_councils/family/documents/ rc_pc_family_doc_20030808_cloning-trujillo_en.html.*

Migliore, Archbishop Celestino. Intervention at the UN on Item 150: "International Convention Against the Reproductive Cloning of Human Beings." October 21, 2004. *www. vatican.va/roman_curia/secretariat_state/2004/documents/ rc_seg-st_20041021_migliore-cloning_en.html.*

Pontifical Academy for Life. *Reflections on Cloning.* www. vatican.va/roman_curia/pontifical_academies/acdlife/documents/ rc_pa_acdlife_doc_30091997_clon_en.html.

The Holy See. *On Human Cloning.* www.vatican.va/roman_ curia/secretariat_state/2004/documents/rc_seg-st_ 20040927_cloning_en.html.

The Holy See. *Observations on the Universal Declaration on the Human Genome and Human Rights.* www.vatican.va/ roman_curia/secretariat_state/documents/rc_seg-st_ 25091998_genoma_en.html.

Documents from USCCB Secretariat of Pro-Life Activities

Alvaré, Helen. *Assisted Reproductive Technology and the Family.* 2007. www.usccb.org/prolife/programs/rlp/Alvare.pdf.

Anderson, Marie, MD, and John Bruchalski, MD. *Assisted Reproductive Technologies Are Anti-Woman.* 2004. www.usccb. org/prolife/programs/rlp/04anderson.shtml.

Coors, Marilyn E. *Genetic Enhancement: Custom Kids and Chimeras.* 2005. www.usccb.org/prolife/programs/rlp/coors05 finaleng.pdf.

Doerflinger, Richard M. *False Freedom and the Culture of Death.* 2000. www.usccb.org/prolife/programs/rlp/00rldoe.shtml.

Doerflinger, Richard M. *Human Experimentation and the Sanctity of Life*. 1985. *www.usccb.org/prolife/issues/fetalresearch/rlpdoerf85.shtml*.

Haas, John M. *Begotten Not Made: A Catholic View of Reproductive Technology*. 1998. *www.usccb.org/prolife/programs/rlp/98rlphaa.shtml*.

Usala, Anton-Lewis, MD. *The Case Against Funding Human Embryonic Stem Cell Research*. 2001. *www.usccb.org/prolife/programs/rlp/01usal.shtml*.